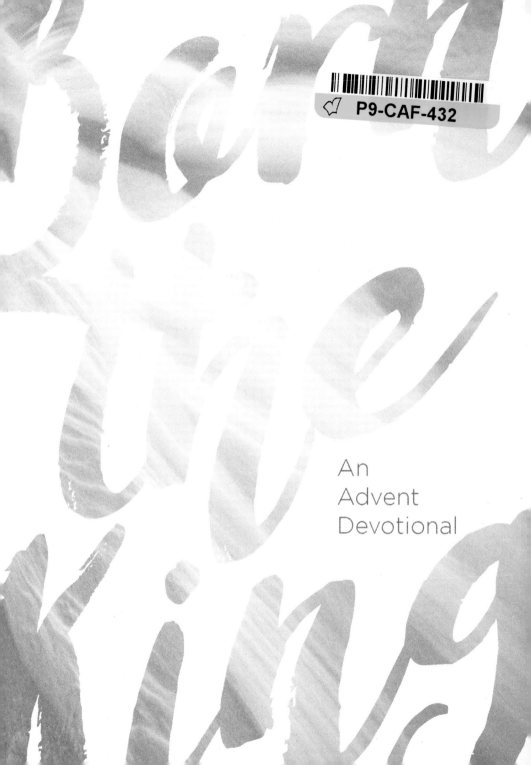

P9-CAF-432

An
Advent
Devotional

Copyright © 2019 by The Foundry Publishing

The Foundry Publishing
PO Box 419527
Kansas City, MO 64141
thefoundrypublishing.com

978-0-8341-3794-3

Printed in the
United States of America

All rights reserved. No part of this publication may be reproduced,
stored in a retrieval system, or transmitted in any form or by any
means—for example, electronic, photocopy, recording—without the
prior written permission of the publisher. The only exception is brief
quotations in printed reviews.

Cover Design: J.R. Caines (Caines Design)
Interior Design: J.R. Caines (Caines Design)/Sharon Page

All Scripture quotations, unless indicated, are taken from The Holy Bible:
New International Version® (NIV®). Copyright © 1973, 1978, 1984, 2011
by Biblica, Inc.® Used by permission of Zondervan. All rights reserved
worldwide.

Scripture quotations marked (NRSV) are from the New Revised Stan-
dard Version Bible, copyright © 1989 the Division of Christian Education
of the National Council of the Churches of Christ in the United States of
America. Used by permission. All rights reserved.

The internet addresses, email addresses, and phone numbers in this
book are accurate at the time of publication. They are provided as a
resource. The Foundry Publishing does not endorse them or vouch for
their content or permanence.

10 9 8 7 6 5 4 3 2 1

REV. CHRISTINE YOUN HUNG is a pastor, writer, speaker, and the director of pastoral development for the Northern California District of the Church of the Nazarene. Prior to joining the Northern California District staff, Christine served as pastor of Trinity Church Rowland Heights Campus, a multisite, multiethnic church serving the Los Angeles area. Christine also served as a missionary teacher in Taipei, Taiwan, for three years. She holds a bachelor's degree in education from the University of Calgary and is currently pursuing her Master of Divinity at Nazarene Theological Seminary. Her innovative approach to group inductive Bible study has been presented at a number of conferences. She has written articles and devotionals for The Foundry Publishing and is a frequent guest speaker at conferences, workshops, college campuses, retreats, and pastor training days. Christine takes deep joy in her husband, Albert, and their four amazing children.

REV. ALBERT HUNG is the district superintendent of the Northern California District of the Church of the Nazarene. He is the first Asian American to hold the position of superintendent in the USA/Canada Region. Prior to his current assignment, Albert served as lead pastor of Trinity Church, a multisite, multiethnic church serving the English, Spanish, Chinese, and Filipino communities east of Los Angeles. He also served as the international chaplain for Azusa Pacific University, leading chapel services for a global community of students from more than thirty countries. After spending several years in the entertainment business as a stage director, recording artist, and television host, Albert received a call from the Lord to pastoral ministry in 2003 while serving as a missionary in Taipei, Taiwan. He speaks frequently on the topics of preaching, cross-cultural ministry, leadership development, and the future of the church. His published work includes articles for *Holiness Today*, *Grace and Peace*, and the *Reflecting God* devotional series.

Table of

Contents

Dear Church,

Participating in the season of Advent is a time-honored tradition that helps embed the gospel story in our hearts. God the Father, in his infinite love and mercy, sent his Son, Jesus Christ, into the world to find the sons and daughters of God and bring them home. He came as a helpless babe, dependent on human hands for his every need. But this was no ordinary child. Jesus was born a King. The champion of heaven had come to lead a revolution against sin and death. He came to open the gates of his Father's kingdom to all. And we have been swept up into this story.

No one really knows when Christians began celebrating the season of Advent, but the tradition dates back to at least AD 567, when the Roman Catholic Church ordered monks to fast every day during December until Christmas. In the nineteenth century, German believers counted down the days to Christmas by marking twenty-four chalk lines on a door and erasing one each day. For centuries, Christians have recognized that making room for Christ in our hearts should be a lengthy, intentional, disciplined process. Participating in this four-week devotional journey is our way of continuing this time-honored tradition of spiritual formation.

All good things take time. We'd like to invite you to spend the next twenty-five days "Adventing" with us. Through prayer, Scripture readings, stories, reflection, dialogue, and opportunities to respond to the Holy Spirit, we will prepare our hearts to receive Christ not only as our Savior but also as our King, so that we might be formed in his likeness and participate more fully in his redemptive work in the world. Since we tend to learn better in community, we encourage you to embark on this journey with family and friends, sharing your insights with each other along the way.

Thank you for allowing us to be part of your lives for the next few weeks. We have been praying for you. May the Lord awaken in you a sense of hope and excitement as you prepare your hearts to celebrate the birth of Christ.

Love,

Christine Youn Hung and Albert Hung

How to use this book

To help you gain the maximum benefit from this devotional experience, we'd like to offer you the following suggestions for engaging with the content you'll find within these pages.

TAKE NOTES. Studies show that we learn better when we write things down. Feel free to mark up this book so you have a record of your time with God. Highlight or underline ideas that challenge your thinking. Take notes and write questions in the margins and white space throughout the book. You'll be encouraged to refer back to your margin musings during the course of our time together.

TALK ABOUT THE EXPERIENCE. At the end of each day, we've included a section titled "Questions for Discussion or Reflection." You can consider them on your own, perhaps as a journaling exercise, but we also suggest using them as conversation starters with others. We think you'll find the experience stimulating and conducive to building deeper relationships.

RESPOND TO GOD. The purpose of a devotional is to increase our devotion to Christ and his kingdom. Each day you will also be invited to bring a gift for the King. We've suggested a simple action you can take to express your love for Jesus and your recognition of his lordship in your life. Some of these actions you can do alone; others will require that you engage with others. Since Jesus tells us that his disciples will be known by their love, these exercises are designed to increase our love for both God and neighbor.

SAVOR GOD'S PROMISES. Meditation is another useful tool for spiritual formation. We've included a daily blessing from Scripture at the end of each devotional. We encourage you to meditate on this verse often throughout the day. Quiet your mind for a moment and repeat the passage a few times, allowing God's words to penetrate your heart. How do God's words make you feel? What does God want you to know? What does God want you to do? Think on these things. Then thank the Lord and continue with your day.

REFLECT ON GOD'S PRESENCE AND ACTIVITY. At the end of each week, you will have an opportunity to write a response to God's activity in your life. Look over your notes and highlights from the past several days. When were you aware of God's presence? What evidence did you see of God's activity in your life? Take some time to write a letter of thanksgiving to the Lord as an act of worship and devotion.

The more you are able to engage with the daily readings and exercises, the more you will gain from our time together. We encourage you, however, to enjoy the journey. Jesus is waiting for you. Let's begin.

The Unexpected Hour

First Sunday of Advent
December 1, 2019

Congregational Prayer

(Leader/**Everyone**)

O Lord, how majestic is your name in all the earth.
We exalt your name above all other names.

You have set your glory above the heavens and established your strength.
We worship you, O Lord, in the beauty of your holiness.

Awaken your people; alert them to their iniquities and shortcomings.
May we be set apart for you, holy and blameless in your sight.

Set your watchmen to stand guard and direct the paths of your people.
May we watch daily at your gates, waiting at your doorposts.

May we commit our spirits to you as we prepare, anticipate, and long for the coming of our King.

Amen

Keep Watch

Sunday, December 1, 2019
CHRISTINE

SCRIPTURE: Matthew 24:36-44

Therefore keep watch, because you do not know on what day your Lord will come.
—Matthew 24:42

Are you ready for Christmas?

It is the first day of December. I'm sure you have already started hearing Christmas tunes, spotting Christmas decorations in stores, and scheduling Christmas events for the weeks ahead. Perhaps stress levels have already been rising as you make mental lists of all the things that need to be done—shopping, card mailing, meal planning, shopping, gift wrapping, tree trimming, shopping, house cleaning, decorating, Christmas performances, and more shopping—in the name of celebrating the birth of Jesus Christ, our Lord and Savior.

In the busyness of planning and preparing, Christmas often creeps up on me. That is to say, come Christmas Day, I have felt . . . nothing. No joy, no peace, no anticipation, and definitely no sense of sacred awe over the reality that the Creator of the universe chose to become a human baby, trading his throne for a manger—just because he loved me.

Almighty God was embodied in flesh and walked in our midst, and I missed the wonder of it all because Christmas became something it wasn't supposed to be. Christmas became a checklist rather than a celebration. Christmas became about pressure rather than peace. It became about commercialism rather than Christ.

If this is the way we squander our Advent season leading up to Christmas, in what posture are we waiting for the second coming of Christ? Are we keeping watch? Are we ready for the coming of the Son of Man? Will we be like the people in the days of Noah, eating turkey, drinking apple cider, being merry and bright, only to be swept away by the flood? Or will we build our lives around the hope of Christ as faithfully as Noah built the ark?

The practice of Advent presents an opportunity for spiritual formation. It is tempting to follow the patterns of this world, especially during Christmas. How can we sanctify our holiday rituals so that they rise above self-indulgence, commercialism, and obligation? How do we transform traditions so that we may honor the birth of our King? Only when we take the necessary time each day to prayerfully reflect on the Lord's presence in our lives can we be drawn into a heartfelt worship where he is exalted in our festivities. Only then can we perceive all the ways the Spirit is inviting us to sit expectantly, adoringly, and hopefully for the coming of the King.

We have twenty-four days in December to prepare our hearts to celebrate the birth of Jesus—and an undisclosed amount of days to prepare our hearts for his second coming. May this Advent season not only prepare him room on Christmas Day but also give him permanent residency in our daily living. May the sacred moments of Advent make way to the building of sacred spaces in our hearts throughout the year—where we are keeping watch for the Lord's return, the day when all of creation will be reconciled to him who was born the King.

Questions for Discussion or Reflection

1. In what ways has Christmas become about anything but celebrating the birth of Christ? How has the church been vulnerable to this temptation?

2. What past practices have helped you acknowledge the awe and wonder of the incarnation of Christ?

3. If this is truly a celebration about the birth of Christ, what do you think Jesus would consider appropriate birthday gifts befitting the Son of God?

4. Describe how the practice of Advent is about preparing our hearts both for the birth of Christ and for the second coming of Jesus.

Gifts for the King

Write down your Christmas to-do list. Think of creative ways to honor Jesus as you complete each item on the list. Commit this to prayer.

_____

_____

_____

_____

_____

_____

_____

_____

_____

_____

Daily Blessing

Come, Lord Jesus. The grace of the Lord Jesus be with God's people. Amen.
—Revelation 22:20b–21

Watchmen

Monday, December 2, 2019
CHRISTINE

SCRIPTURES: Isaiah 52:7–10; 62:6–7; Ezekiel 33:1–6

I have posted watchmen on your walls, Jerusalem; they will never be silent day or night. You who call on the LORD, give yourselves no rest, and give him no rest till he establishes Jerusalem and makes her the praise of the earth.
—Isaiah 62:6–7

Our two oldest children, Eli and Mica, have always been very close. We're pretty sure homeschooling did that. They were each other's favorite playmates for years. They weathered the woes and joys of schooling together, shared all their possessions, and told each other secrets to which even Albert and I are not privy.

I can recall an excursion we had at a playground when they were young. I was with their little sister at the baby swings when my son came running toward me with Mica in tow, tears streaming down her face. Despite Eli's warning to stay clear of the rough group of boys playing tag on the monkey bars, Mica had proceeded to climb up the metal ladder. Sure enough, her vulnerable fingers got caught under someone's sneakers. Mica learned that day to heed her big brother's counsel, and Eli continues to protect her the best he can.

We didn't have to teach Eli to watch over his sister. It was instinctive, a natural outflow of his love for her. In the same way, we are to watch over each other.

Watchmen used to be critical for community safety. They stood vigil on high walls surrounding the city to detect and alert the military to any encroaching dangers. In the Old Testament, God appointed prophets to be the spiritual watchmen for God's people. A prophet discerned God's messages of caution to safeguard the culture from sin and rebellion. The prophet also proclaimed the good news of God's tidings and salvation.

Whom is God appointing you to watch over and protect? Pastors and priests have been ordained to watch over and protect their congregations, but is this responsibility limited only to the clergy office? What about others? What about you? Have you been called?

I believe God calls every one of us—the priesthood of believers—to be watch guards. Whether it is over a whole congregation, your family, your roommates, a small group, or a whole nation, the Lord gives each of us a mission to discern and proclaim the message of God's heart for God's people.

On the other hand, God has also placed watch guards *for* us in our lives. These prophetic voices are often criticized harshly or rejected by those who can't handle God's hard truths. Rather than listening with lament, repentance, and conviction, opponents indignantly try to silence what so urgently needs to be heard. This need to silence a prophetic voice is often due to an unholy obsession with comfort and self-preservation that threatens our ability to maintain a kingdom perspective in earthly matters.

In a 1963 *Time* magazine interview, Karl Barth said he once advised young theologians thus: "Take your Bible and take your newspaper, and read both. But interpret newspapers from your Bible." Through the lens of Scripture, we can discern how to engage with the world as salt and light for the sake of the gospel.

How is God calling you, personally, to boldly speak out, pray for, gently confront, encourage, or alert a loved one? How is the Lord calling you to listen to and ally with those whom God has called to alert God's people? How will you spread the gift of God's goodness and truth this Advent season?

Questions for Discussion or Reflection

1. Whom has the Lord put under your spiritual care and protection?

2. Have you consistently spoken God's truth into the lives with which God has entrusted you? Have you actively participated in their spiritual formation?

3. What is going on in the world right now that needs your attention and care? What are the godly, prophetic voices you need to listen to and consider?

Gifts for the King

As you gather with God's people this Advent season, ask the Lord for wisdom on how to be a voice that directs others to acknowledge God's truth and love.

Daily Blessing

Go and make disciples of all nations . . . teaching them to obey everything I have commanded you. And surely I am with you always, to the very end of the age.
—Matthew 28:19–20

Watch and Pray

Tuesday, December 3, 2019

CHRISTINE

SCRIPTURE: Matthew 26:36-41

Watch and pray so that you will not fall into temptation. The spirit is willing, but the flesh is weak.
—Matthew 26:41

There are two moments in Scripture when the humanity of Jesus is the most profoundly exposed. One is at his birth; the other is during his deep anguish in the garden of Gethsemane.

It is hard to comprehend that God—who formed the first human from the dust of the earth—also chose to be formed in the womb of his own creation. Mighty God—incarnated as a newborn baby—cried, slept, cooed, and nursed in the arms of a woman. How vulnerable and how very mortal is this image of God as helpless babe.

In the garden of Gethsemane, Jesus again appears to be vulnerable and extremely mortal as he pleads with the Father. He seeks an alternative to the suffering on the cross for the redemption of humanity. As he struggles between flesh and spirit, we see Jesus's faithfulness and love shine through in his darkest moment. He ultimately submits to the Father but not without baring his human heart first. The agony and grief are more than he can shoulder on his own, so Jesus turns to his dearest friends for support, asking them to "watch and pray."

The glorified Christ persists in the same manner now; he asks us, his beloved friends, to watch and pray; to be broken over the things that break his heart; to be grieved about the things that grieve him; and then to be moved to prayer, seeking his counsel regarding how we are to respond to such things.

As followers of Jesus, are we willing to accompany him to the garden of Gethsemane? Are we willing to bear the heaviness of his sadness and grief? The disciples could barely stay awake as Jesus prayed into the night. I am convinced they were not aware of the depth of pain their Master was experiencing. If they understood what was to come, if they comprehended the burden that was to be borne, I imagine their prayers would have persevered through the night.

But we stand on the other side of the cross. We know what is at stake. The Spirit of the Lord is in us, and if we only took the time to hear and feel and respond through this Spirit, we would not fall asleep. We would not turn off the news with a mere shaking of the head or clicking of our tongues. We would not walk away from the homeless family without giving more than a raised eyebrow and a shrug of indifference. We would not shrug at the state of the affairs of our country and turn a blind eye to the corruption of our leaders.

Too many times I have heard Christians say, "I don't watch the news anymore—it's too depressing," or, "Can we please not talk about politics in church anymore? I just want to hear about the love of Jesus!" Or, "The spiritual state of my family member, or neighbor, or friend, has nothing to do with me; religion is a personal matter."

As the church, we need to wake up, watch, and pray. God, grant us grace to filter everything through the heart of Jesus. Grant us courage to go about our Father's business with the same compassion and determination Jesus showed in the garden.

Questions for Discussion or Reflection

1. Have you fallen asleep at the command "watch and pray"? In what ways have you been tempted to retreat away from the world and live in a Christian bubble?

2. What grieves the heart of Jesus? What grieves you? How much cross-over is there?

3. How have you engaged with the darkness of this world as the light of Jesus?

Gifts for the King

Spend time with Jesus and accompany him in the garden of Gethsemane. Ask him to bring a person or circumstance to mind that he cares about. Feel his heart toward this person or circumstance. Ask him how you should respond and take action.

Daily Blessing

May the God of hope fill you with all joy and peace as you trust in him, so that you may overflow with hope by the power of the Holy Spirit.
—Romans 15:13

Watchful and Thankful

Wednesday, December 4, 2019
CHRISTINE

SCRIPTURES: Colossians 4:2; Hebrews 12:26–29

Devote yourselves to prayer, being watchful and thankful.
—Colossians 4:2

Therefore, since we are receiving a kingdom that cannot be shaken, let us be thankful, and so worship God acceptably with reverence and awe.
—Hebrews 12:28

Earthquakes are frightening because of their unpredictability. It is impossible to tell if the shaking will cease or continue on to catastrophic levels of devastation.

Once I was on the eleventh floor during an earthquake in Taiwan, where buildings are intentionally designed to sway back and forth to absorb the shock in the event of an earthquake. I sat in a corner, praying frantically to be rescued as my apartment heaved and shuddered. I was convinced that this was the last moment of my life. I heard shouts out in the hallway as people ran down the emergency exits, but I was frozen to the spot. Fear had gripped me. It was the first earthquake I had ever experienced.

Everyone ran out of the building—but Albert ran in. He was just returning from the market when the earthquake started. Disregarding any danger to himself, he sprinted up eleven flights of stairs to come back for me. The apartment did not topple over, and Albert and I did not die in that earthquake. But I did learn something that day. I learned that Albert loved me enough to put his own life in danger to rescue me. He came back for me. I also learned the value of knowing that my life is in the Lord's hands. I learned that his faithfulness is unshakable, even when the world seems to be crumbling down around us.

The author of Hebrews tells us that a shaking of the earth and the heavens will take place at the end of time. We can argue about whether this description is literal or figurative, but the author makes one thing clear: the things of this world will not remain, and the kingdom of God will not be shaken. As citizens of God's kingdom, for this we should be thankful.

As we are called to watch and pray, we may face moments of discouragement. We may feel overwhelmed by the wickedness and injustices of this world. Our prayers may not seem to make a difference. Our messages of hope may seem to fall on deaf ears. Our efforts to minister to those who are hurting or sick or lonely may seem to bear little fruit. Our circumstances may be shaky and unpredictable, testing our faith.

May the beauty and awe of Christ's birth renew your hope and your faith this season—even if the world seems to be crumbling down. The birth of Jesus was a flicker of hope for God's people facing difficult and desperate times. The same is true for us. It is a flicker of hope promising that God's steadfast love will see us through the circumstances we are facing; that the kingdom of God is unshakeable; that Jesus gave up his life to rescue us; and that Jesus is coming back for us.

Questions for Discussion or Reflection

1. What circumstances in your life challenge your faith the most?

2. What does the birth of Christ mean to you? What promises are confirmed through his birth?

3. Why should we be thankful that the kingdom we are receiving cannot be shaken?

Gifts for the King

Spend some time worshiping the King today. Sing songs of worship and exalt his name in prayer, while reflecting on all the reasons you are thankful for him.

Daily Blessing

Wait for the LORD; be strong and take heart and wait for the LORD.
—Psalm 27:14

The Armor of Light

Thursday, December 5, 2019

CHRISTINE

SCRIPTURES: Romans 13:11–14; 1 Thessalonians 5:8

The night is nearly over; the day is almost here. So let us put aside the deeds of darkness and put on the armor of light.
—*Romans 13:12*

Why does being bad feel so good?

You may have wrestled with the temptation to do the very things that later bring feelings of remorse, distress, and guilt. It is perplexing. Why are we inclined to repeat behaviors that violate our moral code, damage our self-image, or hurt the people we love? There is something at the very moment of wrongdoing that temporarily satisfies an unholy hunger. Perhaps it's a thrill, a high, an escape, or a reprieve. Our cravings stir deeper and stronger—even stronger than the guilt that often ensues—and we find ourselves in a cycle of sin.

The desires of the flesh are caused by the separation between God and humanity. We were created to be in deep relationship with God, but sin created a great divide. There is a hunger in our bones that can only be sated by the love of Jesus, yet we deceive ourselves and turn to other things, searching for something better. But there is nothing better than, nothing that satisfies like, the love of the Lord.

Paul the apostle encouraged his people to lay aside their deeds of darkness and put on the armor of light. We've become accustomed to such imagery, but if we pause to think about it, "the armor of light" is quite a peculiar phrase. What *is* an armor of light, and how does one put it on? How could it possibly protect one? What does the phrase even mean?

We took our kids into a cave during one of our family trips. In the deepest part of the cave, the tour guide shut off all the lights, and we turned off our flashlights. I had never been in such absolute darkness. I couldn't even see my hand in front of my face. I shuddered at the thought of being lost in the twists and turns of the cave without a flashlight. Undoubtedly, there is nothing more beautiful to see than light when you are lost in darkness. It is the way out. It is freedom.

Likewise, the armor of light illuminates the path of darkness. It reveals truth and points to the way out. We are able to see with clarity the things that lead to destruction and the things of God that give us eternal joy.

There have been many circumstances in my life when earthly reason seemed to justify an unholy response. *I shouldn't forgive him. I want her to feel bad for what she did. I should not give them a second, or even third, chance.* I have felt entitled to raw, unfiltered reactions when I am not at my best. I could go for days and days with a smug attitude, believing myself to be in the right.

Spending time with Jesus changes all that. When I am at his feet in humble posture, clothed in the Lord's armor of light, my thoughts start to shift toward the ways of Jesus. When we listen for God's voice through prayer, Scripture, and worship, the path of righteousness is lit, and the power and protection of the Lord loosen the foothold of darkness in our lives.

Questions for Discussion or Reflection

1. What sorts of vices keep you from a vibrant relationship with Jesus?

2. Are there areas in your life that you intentionally keep darkened and hidden away, lest you feel the conviction to change and surrender?

3. What are the moments in your past when you have felt the deepest satisfaction in the Lord?

Gifts for the King

Allow the King to examine your heart and reveal any sin in your life. Reflect deeply on each revealed sin and the ways it impacts you and your relationships with God and with others. Surrender each sin to the Lord and pray that the light of Jesus would bring clarity and truth.

Daily Blessing

The rising sun will come to us from heaven to shine on those living in darkness and in the shadow of death, to guide our feet into the path of peace.
—Luke 1:78b–79

Blameless

Friday, December 6, 2019
CHRISTINE

SCRIPTURE: Philippians 1:9-11; 1 Thessalonians 5:23-24

May God himself, the God of peace, sanctify you through and through. May your whole spirit, soul and body be kept blameless at the coming of our Lord Jesus Christ. The one who calls you is faithful, and he will do it.
—1 Thessalonians 5:23-24

When I was a child, my relationship with God was often fraught with shame and guilt. I viewed our heavenly Father as a temperamental parent and myself as the object of his constant displeasure. I ached to please him, but I felt like I constantly fell short. I wanted so much to draw close to him, but I didn't believe I was worthy. I felt little joy or comfort in God's presence. A relationship with God was too difficult to sustain.

As an adult, I sometimes catch myself falling into similar patterns. I have tasted the goodness of the Lord. I have experienced his amazing grace. I have felt his boundless love. Yet there are moments when the shadow of that little girl reappears, and I severely berate myself for my spiritual deficiency. John of the Cross, a Carmelite monk during the sixteenth century, would call this response pride. He believed we should be content in our spiritual poverty, trusting the Lord's faithfulness to sanctify us through and through, in his perfect timing. Our impatience and anger—aimed at ourselves for not being more saintlike—demonstrate an unwillingness to submit to God's process of transformation for us.

God could eliminate our desire to sin with the snap of a finger. In his wisdom, he doesn't. God's method is often slow, drawing us into a deeper dependence on his Spirit and strength, giving us reason to savor his love for us—a love we haven't earned (and never could earn). And the grace of the Lord is magnified before our very eyes.

Now I have an internal script to combat the messages of shame whenever I mess up. It goes something like this: *Yes, you messed up again. Go to the Lord with a contrite spirit, and he will forgive you. The Lord has not completed his work in that particular area of your life yet. Be patient. He will. He knows what he is doing. It is the Lord's labor of love. Do you feel his fingers molding you to his likeness? There is no shame. You are in God's hands. There is only love. There is only grace.* It took many years for the Lord to rewrite my internal script. As your love overflows with more knowledge and insight, I pray that your internal script is being rewritten as well.

Especially as you're Adventing, reflect deeply on the implications of the incarnation of Christ. God became human. From this came the most profound union, demonstrating God's unfathomable love for you. It is a union in the flesh—Christ died for all of humanity—and a union in the spirit— Christ continues his work in us, making us pure and blameless.

Questions for Discussion or Reflection

1. What internal voices do you hear when you fall into sin?

2. How should the birth of Jesus impact the way you see yourself?

3. How is God's Spirit working in us to make us pure and blameless?

Gifts for the King

Spend time with the King today and ask him how he feels about you. Let this determine your internal script in moments of shame.

_____

_____

_____

_____

_____

_____

_____

_____

Daily Blessing

Praise be to the Lord, the God of Israel, because he has come to his people and redeemed them.
—Luke 1:68

Responding to the King

Saturday, December 7, 2019

Look over your notes and highlights from this week's devotionals. What do you sense God saying to you? How do you think God is asking you to respond? What evidence do you see of God's activity in your life this week? Take some time to write a letter of response and thanksgiving to the Lord as an act of worship and devotion.

Dear Heavenly Father,

Daily Blessing

The Lord bless you and keep you; the Lord make his face shine on you and be gracious to you; the Lord turn his face toward you and give you peace.
—Numbers 6:24–26

The Kingdom of Heaven Is Near

Second Sunday of Advent
December 8, 2019

Congregational Prayer

(Leader/**Everyone**)

O Christ, our Lord,
Our Redeemer and Friend,
You bring good news for all people, everywhere.

Your kingdom is near.
Heaven is coming.
Help us to make a straight path for you,
That we may be your people,
That you may be our God.

You are the Son of God.
You are the Light of the world.
You are the Bread of life.
You are the Good Shepherd.
You are the Resurrection and the Life.

We acknowledge you, O Lord.
We welcome you in this place.
Fill our hearts with hope and expectation.
Increase our faith and give us courage.
Move us to love our neighbors in your name.

Lead on, King Jesus.

Amen

In Keeping with Repentance

Sunday, December 8, 2019

ALBERT

SCRIPTURE: Matthew 3:1–12

In those days John the Baptist came, preaching in the wilderness of Judea and saying, "Repent, for the kingdom of heaven has come near."
—Matthew 3:1

John the Baptist preached in the wilderness of Judea, calling people to repent and prepare for the coming of the Lord. How do we prepare ourselves to receive our king? What does a repentant heart look like?

People came from all around the Jordan to see John in the wilderness. They left their places of comfort to embark on a spiritual pilgrimage. There, they confessed their sins, naming their failure to live up to God's standards in the presence of others. They asked John to baptize them in the river in a ritual act of cleansing and the hope of restoration. These are the actions of a repentant and expectant people, awaiting their king.

Yet when John saw the Pharisees and Sadducees approaching, he rebuked them and issued a stern warning: "Produce fruit in keeping with repentance. The ax is already at the root of the trees, and every tree that does not produce good fruit will be cut down and thrown into the fire" (Matthew 3:8, 10).

John came as a witness to testify that "the true light that gives light to everyone [Christ] was coming into the world" (John 1:9). Jesus came to give sight to the blind so that we might see God as he truly is and ourselves as we truly are. That's what light does: it reveals what is true while exposing what is false.

We can have the appearance of faith without any meaningful relationship with God. We can follow the letter of the law while violating the spirit of the law. We can talk the talk without walking the walk. We can enjoy the trappings of Christmas without worshiping the Christ child. What did John see in the Pharisees and Sadducees that caused him to warn them to examine their hearts and their behavior? What does Jesus see in us? Do we approach Jesus with a humble and contrite spirit, ready to confront our true nature, confess our sins, and invite God to give us a new heart?

John baptized with water, but Jesus baptizes us with the Holy Spirit and with fire. He not only lifts the penalty of sin, but he also liberates us from the power of sin. This is the King who has come to rescue his people. This is Christ, the Son of God. Repent, and believe this good news!

Questions for Discussion or Reflection

1. What is meant by John the Baptist's warning to produce fruit in keeping with repentance? How might these words apply to your own life?

2. John said that, while he baptized with water, Jesus would baptize with the Holy Spirit and with fire. What is the difference between the two? Would you say that you've experienced baptism of the Holy Spirit? Why or why not?

3. Jesus is "the true light that gives light to everyone." In what ways has God helped you acknowledge the truth about your own condition—perhaps regarding your strengths and weaknesses, your calling in life, or areas where you need to repent and grow?

Gifts for the King

Ignatius of Loyola developed what he called spiritual exercises to regulate and develop one's interior life with Christ. In particular, the prayer of examen has become a vital tool in developing greater awareness of God's presence and activity in our lives. A quick online search will result in many examples of how to practice a prayer of examen. Spend 5–10 minutes praying using the following pattern as a way to make a straight path for the Lord to work in your life.

Part 1: Awareness of God

- Be still. Close your eyes, quiet your mind, and become aware of God's presence.
- Review. Think back to the events of the past twenty-four hours. When, where, and how did God reveal his presence to you? How did you respond in these moments?
- Give thanks. Offer prayers of gratitude to God for his activity in your life.

Part 2: Awareness of Self

- Reflect. What are you thinking and feeling? What is the state of your mind and spirit in this moment? Over the past twenty-four hours?
- Invite. Using the words of Psalm 139, ask the Lord to reveal any un-Christlike attitudes or behaviors: "Search me, God, and know my heart; test me and know my anxious thoughts. See if there is any offensive way in me, and lead me in the way everlasting" (Psalm 139:23–24).

Part 3: Prayer of Expectation

- Pray. What do you hope and expect that God will do in the hours ahead? Reaffirm your trust in his love, wisdom, and promises.

Daily Blessing

But when he, the Spirit of truth, comes, he will guide you into all the truth. He will not speak on his own; he will speak only what he hears, and he will tell you what is yet to come.
—John 16:13

The Time Has Come

Monday, December 9, 2019

ALBERT

SCRIPTURES: Mark 1:15; Revelation 9:20-21

"The time has come," he said. "The kingdom of God has come near. Repent and believe the good news!"
—Mark 1:15

Christians are often accused of being close-minded. While we may often act in a manner deserving of this label, one cannot be a true disciple of Jesus without an openness to change and new ideas. Jesus could not have been clearer when he said, "Very truly I tell you, no one can see the kingdom of God unless they are born again" (John 3:3). He also explained, "Unless you change and become like little children, you will never enter the kingdom of heaven" (Matthew 18:3).

God's love is unconditional. Salvation is offered to all, no matter how deep our transgressions. There is a place in God's family for all who receive Christ the King, the Word made flesh. But to enter the kingdom of God, we must first repent and believe the good news. We must lay down our pride, our rights, our allegiances, and even our loves so that the Spirit may do its work in us. Repentance is not about remorse. Repentance is about change. To repent is to change our minds, our attitudes, our loyalties, our words, our behaviors—indeed, the entire sum and trajectory of our lives. Jesus does not intend to make us better people; he intends to make us entirely *different* people. Christ is making all things new, starting with us.

The Lord reveals to John in Revelation that, when Christ returns to judge the nations, there will be those who stubbornly cling to their old ways of life. They will not stop worshiping idols, nor will they repent of their evil deeds. But we, sisters and brothers, are called to a different path. We are disciples of Jesus. The apostle Paul urges us to renounce our former ways, saying, "You were taught, with regard to your former way of life, to put off your old self, which is being corrupted by its deceitful desires; to be made new in the attitude of your minds; and to put on the new self, created to be like God in true righteousness and holiness" (Ephesians 4:22–24).

The period between Thanksgiving and Christmas has become a time of spending and consumption in American culture. We buy gifts for family and friends, often throwing in a few for ourselves as well. What might happen if we also took time to empty our lives of un-Christlike attitudes and behaviors? What if we took seriously the call to repentance and believed the good news that Jesus is Lord and that his kingdom is near?

When someone becomes a U.S. citizen, they are required to make the following statement: "I hereby declare, on oath, that I absolutely and entirely renounce and abjure all allegiance and fidelity to any foreign prince, potentate, state, or sovereignty, of whom or which I have heretofore been a subject or citizen." In the same way, when we become followers of Jesus, we renounce all other allegiances and come under the authority of a new king. In the words of the apostle Paul, "Our citizenship is in heaven. And we eagerly await a Savior from there, the Lord Jesus Christ" (Philippians 3:20). Become like a little child, as if you were learning everything for the first time, and allow the Lord to teach you what it means to live as a citizen of heaven.

Questions for Discussion or Reflection

1. When we become disciples of Jesus, we enter into a lifelong process of learning and change. What was one of the first things that the Lord led you to change about your attitudes, behaviors, or lifestyle?

2. In what ways is the Lord calling you to change in this season of your life, so that you might look more like Jesus and do his work in the world? What is God asking you to stop doing? What is God asking you to start doing?

Gifts for the King

Pray for the Holy Spirit to help you simplify your life so that you may devote more of your time and energy to loving, serving, and enjoying God. Afterward, collect new or gently used items in your home that might bless someone in need and donate them to a local shelter or thrift store.

Daily Blessing

May God himself, the God of peace, sanctify you through and through. May your whole spirit, soul and body be kept blameless at the coming of our Lord Jesus Christ.
—1 Thessalonians 5:23

Seek First His Kingdom

Tuesday, December 10, 2019
ALBERT

SCRIPTURE: Matthew 6:25-34

For the pagans run after all these things, and your heavenly Father knows that you need them. But seek first his kingdom and his righteousness, and all these things will be given to you as well.
—Matthew 6:32-33

From the moment we wake each morning, we are faced with one choice after another. What should I wear? What will I eat? What should I do? Where will I go? With whom will I spend my time? How should I spend my money? It's estimated that the average adult makes approximately 35,000 conscious decisions every day. That means that, over the season of Advent, you will make approximately 850,000 decisions. Sounds overwhelming, doesn't it? Jesus wasn't kidding when he said, "Do not worry about tomorrow, for tomorrow will worry about itself. Each day has enough trouble of its own" (Matthew 6:34).

We're not always aware of the thoughts and desires that drive our decisions. Different people make different choices and lead vastly different lives. But inside every person is a void that only God can fill. We were made for relationship with our Creator. We intuitively seek him even when we don't know it. Our need for community, our search for significance, our pursuit of joy, our appreciation of beauty, and our desire for justice are all things that are uniquely human longings. They are characteristics of our Creator, in whose image we are made; therefore, we seek to experience these things in our own lives.

Most of us settle for lesser versions of what God created us to enjoy. We settle for material wealth when God offers us spiritual riches. We settle for temporary pleasures when God offers us lasting joy. We settle for human recognition when God offers us divine glory. But Jesus tells us to make seeking our heavenly Father's kingdom and righteousness our first and highest priority. Our Father knows what we need. He will provide for his children. We can live free from worry, knowing that God will care for us.

Making room for Christ's presence and power in our lives requires making hard choices. Often the hardest choices are not between what is good and what is evil but between what is good and what is best. What is the best way for a follower of Jesus to start the day? What is the best way to care for our bodies, which have become a temple for God's Spirit? What is the best way to manage our resources so that, having all we need, we may share with others and "enlarge the harvest of our righteousness" (2 Corinthians 9:10–11)? Our deepest longings are most fully met when God becomes our first love and his agenda our highest priority.

"You will seek me and find me when you seek me with all your heart," the Lord said to the Israelites (Jeremiah 29:13). The same invitation is extended to every individual through the continued witness of the church. But Christmas is when we remember that God, too, is seeking us. Jesus "came to seek and to save the lost" (Luke 19:10). We who are in Christ no longer need to seek the Father. We have been found. We are in Christ, and he is in us. All that remains is to seek the fulfillment of his kingdom on earth, in his name and in his power. So, dear friends, what will you choose to do with the time God has given you? What will you seek first today?

Questions for Discussion or Reflection

1. What are some of the things you commonly worry about? How do you usually deal with worry and anxiety? What alternative strategies have you considered?

2. What is one difficult choice that you are facing right now? How will you decide what to do? What do you think God might be saying to you in light of today's devotional?

3. What does it mean to seek first the kingdom of God? How do we do this in a practical sense?

Gifts for the King

How do you want to start your day tomorrow? What will you seek first? Give some thought to how you will spend your first waking moments each morning. Then plan accordingly. For example, if you'd like to begin by reading Scripture, plan what passages you will read and place your Bible strategically so it's the first thing you see. If you'd like to begin the day with a run, set out your workout clothes and shoes before you go to bed.

Daily Blessing

You will seek me and find me when you seek me with all your heart.
—Jeremiah 29:13

In Your Midst

Wednesday, December 11, 2019
ALBERT

SCRIPTURE: Luke 17:20–21

Once, on being asked by the Pharisees when the kingdom of God would come, Jesus replied, "The coming of the kingdom of God is not something that can be observed, nor will people say, 'Here it is,' or 'There it is,' because the kingdom of God is in your midst."
—Luke 17:20–21

Two summers ago, I came dangerously close to permanently losing vision in one of my eyes. I was working in the garage when I noticed a bungee cord that had become entangled under some junk. Rather than taking the time to sort through the mess, I impatiently tried to yank the cord free. On the third tug, I heard a snapping sound, followed by exploding pain in my right eye. The end of the bungee cord had shot straight into my pupil, instantly filling it with blood. Christine rushed me to the emergency room, where I was told I had sustained serious trauma that would require immediate medical attention (which was rather obvious to me). Thankfully, the doctors were able to save my eyesight, but it took almost three months to recover from my foolish accident.

We depend on our eyesight for so many things: to get around, to do our work, to create beauty, to relate to the world around us. We trust our eyes so much that sometimes we have trouble trusting in things we cannot see. But Jesus tells us that the kingdom of God, though it cannot be physically observed, is in our midst. The kingdom of God is not a metaphor. One day, God's kingdom will be revealed in all its glory when Christ returns. Heaven will be a visible and tangible reality. But that time has not yet come. The kingdom is both here and not here. We see it in part but not in its entirety. We recognize the presence and activity of our King not by looking for signs and wonders in the physical realm but by paying attention to God's work in our spirits and in the spirits of our neighbors.

What is God saying to you during this season of anticipation? What is God doing inside you? How is God working in the lives of your family members and friends? Can you perceive the unseen beauty of the Spirit's movement in the world? When Christ came into the world, not everyone recognized him. Some saw a child. Others saw a king. Some saw a teacher. Others saw the face of God. What do you see?

The kingdom of heaven is in your midst. Pay attention to the little things. Be present in your relationships. Practice mindfulness in the daily rhythms of your life. Ask the Lord to give you eyes to see and ears to hear. God is with us!

Questions for Discussion or Reflection

1. What are some things of great value that cannot typically be seen with the naked eye?

2. Jesus said that the kingdom of God is in our midst. What did he mean?

3. Think about some of the descriptions given in the Scriptures about the coming kingdom of God. What aspects of God's kingdom are most appealing to you, and why?

Gifts for the King

Spend some time today in solitude with the Lord. Sit in silence for ten minutes, paying attention to the inner dynamics of your heart. Listen for the Spirit's voice and allow the Lord to direct your attention where he wills. Do not hide from God. Allow your true self to surface during this time—the good *and* the bad. Respond to God in prayer.

Daily Blessing

The Lord, your God, is in your midst, a warrior who gives victory; he will rejoice over you with gladness, he will renew you in his love; he will exult over you with loud singing.
—Zephaniah 3:17, NRSV

One Such Child

Thursday, December 12, 2019

ALBERT

SCRIPTURES: Matthew 18:1–5; 19:14

Therefore, whoever takes the lowly position of this child is the greatest in the kingdom of heaven. And whoever welcomes one such child in my name welcomes me.
—Matthew 18:4–5

Jesus had a special place in his heart for children. He welcomed them into his presence. He held them up as an example for his disciples to follow. He gives them a place of honor in the kingdom of God. Why does our Lord love children so much, and what can we learn from them?

On one hand, Jesus tells us that we must become like children, taking a posture of humility and dependence on our heavenly Father. In a culture that idolizes individual achievement and self-gratification, we struggle to acknowledge our need for God and others. But those who come to Jesus with open palms and open hearts find that our Lord is gentle, loving, and generous.

We think of Christmas as a season of giving. In reality, it is the season of receiving. God gave the gift of his Son to a hurting and broken world so that we who were dead in our transgressions might rise to new life. He gives us the Holy Spirit to guide and empower us to lead holy and fruitful lives. Children should not feel ashamed to ask their parents for whatever they need: food, clothing, shelter, love. In the same way, God desires that we come to him without fear or doubt, secure in his affections and care for us. We who have received Christ, who have believed in his name, have been given the right to become children of God and call him Father (John 1:12). To enter the kingdom, we must become like little children.

On the other hand, we are also called to protect children, to welcome them and remove any barriers to faith in Christ and participation in God's family. In many ways, children represent those who have little status or power in the world. But our God is a God of justice. He instructs his people to take up the cause of the weakest members of society: the widows, the orphans, the poor, the foreigners. In an article for *Relevant Magazine* called "What Is Biblical Justice?" Tim Keller observes, "In premodern, agrarian societies, these four groups had no social power. They lived at subsistence level and were only days from starvation if there was any famine, invasion or even minor social unrest. Today, this quartet would be expanded to include the refugee, the migrant worker, the homeless and many single parents and elderly people."

The season of Advent reminds us of our sacred responsibility to bring those on the margins into the community of faith. Jesus called a child to him and *placed the child among the disciples.* Whom does God want to place in our midst today? In what ways are we hindering the least of these from full membership and participation in the body of Christ?

Questions for Discussion or Reflection

1. Who is someone in your life who belongs to a marginalized group and is an example of Christlikeness? What have you learned from them?

2. Who is someone who belongs to a marginalized group whom God is calling you to welcome? Why does the kingdom belong to such people?

Gifts for the King

Do you know which people are among the most vulnerable segments of the population in your city? If not, do some research to find out. Talk to your pastor, community leaders, or social agencies in your neighborhood. Then pray about how God might use you to advocate for those on the margins so that all might share in the resources and benefits that society offers.

Daily Blessing

For you have been my hope, Sovereign LORD, my confidence since my youth. From birth I have relied on you; you brought me forth from my mother's womb. I will ever praise you.
—Psalm 71:5-6

Do You Not Perceive It?

Friday, December 13, 2019

ALBERT

SCRIPTURES: Isaiah 43:18–19; 2 Corinthians 5:16–17; Revelation 21:1–27

See, I am doing a new thing! Now it springs up; do you not perceive it? I am making a way in the wilderness and streams in the wasteland.
—Isaiah 43:19

Advent is not just a time to reflect on the wonder of Jesus's birth. Philip H. Pfatteicher notes in his 2013 book, *Journey into the Heart of God*, that "since the time of Bernard of Clairvaux (d. 1153), Christians have spoken of the three comings of Christ: in the flesh in Bethlehem, in our hearts daily, and in glory at the end of time." We are always celebrating what God has done, what God is doing, and what God will do. God is both the author and hero of our story, our captain and our companion, our beginning and our end. He crowns us with glory and shares all that he has with us. John's vision of the world to come reveals God's desire for humanity: that we might be his people, that he might dwell with us and be our God.

One day, Christ will return to set things right. The world will once again be as it should be. There will be no more crying, sickness, pain, death. No more injustice. No more hate, no more division, no more racism or fear or misogyny or prejudice. The "old order of things" will have "passed away" (Revelation 21:4). All will be made new.

That day is coming soon, but it has not arrived yet. Until then, God has appointed us to be a picture and a preview of the coming kingdom. We are to light a path to Jesus and provide a glimpse of heaven through acts of love, charity, and kindness. God says that in his kingdom there will be no more sickness or pain or death. How can we make this world look more like that? God says that in his kingdom there will be no hunger or thirst or poverty. How can we make this world look more like that? God says that in his kingdom there will be no more division, no more hate. How can we make this world look more like that?

We begin by asking God to give us the mind of Christ so that we may know what God is thinking, hear what God is saying, and join in what God is doing. Paul tells us that "from now on we regard no one from a worldly point of view. . . . If anyone is in Christ, the new creation has come. The old has gone, the new is here!" (2 Corinthians 5:16–17). As ambassadors of Christ and citizens of the kingdom, we must learn to think, see, and hear as Jesus does.

We hope and pray that people might see Christ in us. But equally important is whether we are able to see Christ in them. Every person is made in the image of God. Every person has dignity and worth. Every person deserves to be loved. Many are still far from God, lost in their sins, and have yet to experience redemption. But God is at work.

God gives us the ability to see the world both as it is and as it one day will be. We can acknowledge the broken state of affairs around us while working to make earth look more like heaven. One thing we can be sure of is that we are not alone. God is with us. Jesus—who is the same yesterday, today, and forever (see Hebrews 13:8)—continues to come into our hearts daily, even as we wait for him to come in glory at the end of time.

Questions for Discussion or Reflection

1. How has the church historically worked to make the world look a little bit more like heaven? In what areas do we still have a lot of work to do?

2. Think of a time when you misjudged someone. What were your initial impressions, and what made you see that person differently?

Gifts for the King

Take some time to review the major news events of the day. Then reflect on which of them is moving you to prayer. Pray for the people who have been impacted by this event and ask for God to redeem the situation for good.

_____

_____

_____

_____

_____

_____

_____

_____

_____

_____

Daily Blessing

He who was seated on the throne said, "I am making everything new!" Then he said, "Write this down, for these words are trustworthy and true."
—Revelation 21:5

Responding to the King

Saturday, December 14, 2019

Look over your notes and highlights from this week's devotionals. What do you sense God saying to you? How do you think God is asking you to respond? What evidence do you see of God's activity in your life this week? Take some time to write a letter of response and thanksgiving to the Lord as an act of worship and devotion.

Dear Heavenly Father,

Daily Blessing

Peter replied, "Repent and be baptized, every one of you, in the name of Jesus Christ for the forgiveness of your sins. And you will receive the gift of the Holy Spirit. The promise is for you and your children and for all who are far off—for all whom the Lord our God will call."
—Acts 2:38-39

Good
News to
the Poo

Third Sunday of Advent
December 15, 2019

Congregational Prayer

(Leader/**Everyone**)

O Lord, our God, you have chosen to make yourself known
Through your creation, your Word, your Son, and your Spirit.
Now reveal your glory to us and through us, the church.

Speak to us, form us, lead us, dwell in us.
Teach us today how to love as Jesus loves:
To welcome the stranger, heal the sick, and care for the poor;
To bear good news, build bridges, and bring your people home.

For Christ in us is the hope of glory.
May your perfect will prevail in us this day,
In the name of the Father, Son, and Holy Spirit.

Amen

The Deeds of the Messiah

Sunday, December 15, 2019

CHRISTINE

SCRIPTURE: Matthew 11:2–11

When John, who was in prison, heard about the deeds of the Messiah, he sent his disciples to ask him, "Are you the one who is to come, or should we expect someone else?"
—Matthew 11:2–3

Even in the womb, John the Baptist could sense the presence of the Lord draw close as Mary shared the news about her pregnancy with his mother, Elizabeth. In the desert, he lived with a singular focus, proclaiming the message of the kingdom of heaven to prepare the way for the Lord. In the Jordan River, he stood before the Messiah and baptized him with water. Before his very eyes, the heavens opened, and a magnificent triune interplay unfolded as the Spirit descended upon the Son and the Father claimed Jesus as his own.

Yet John the Baptist doubted whether Jesus was indeed the one who was to come. Frankly, who could blame him? He was sitting in prison on death row. He had committed his life to being the Lord's prophet yet now faced execution on King Herod's orders. Where was the divine cavalry? Where was the Messiah? The Savior? The Son of God? Surely, the almighty King himself would come to the rescue! It would seem, however, that evil was winning. This was not at all what John had expected.

How tempting it is to fall into the same doubts, especially in those vulnerable moments when it seems like evil is winning and Jesus is not meeting our expectations. Where is Jesus while suffering and wickedness run rampant around us? Where is the army of God? Where is the overthrowing of darkness?

I recall the days after our first miscarriage, during which I questioned whether Jesus was enough. I was angry and hurt that the Lord had allowed it to happen. At about the same time of my own surgery, our dog, Sasha, also underwent surgery. She had a tubal ligation and several teeth taken out. With stitches along her belly, her jaw numb, and a plastic cone around her head, Sasha had no idea why she was made to suffer so. But I could tell from her big round eyes and the way she crawled up in my lap that she trusted me. In her heart, she knew everything was all right in the world because I was there.

The Lord spoke to me through Sasha: *Can you hear and see the faithfulness of the Lord throughout your life? Can you trust me, as Sasha trusts you, even in your suffering? Even when life doesn't turn out as expected?*

Likewise, Jesus sent messengers to John to report to him what they heard and saw. Perhaps John, like many others in his time, expected Jesus to overthrow the oppressive powers that afflicted them. Instead, the deeds of the Messiah were to minister to people one by one as he healed, restored, and blessed. He was overturning darkness by means other than force and violence. He loved people into the kingdom of God. He loved them into the freedom that comes with knowing that Jesus is Lord. He loved them beyond their wildest expectations.

These deeds of Jesus were so numerous "that even the whole world would not have room for the books that would be written" (John 21:25). He continues to perform these wondrous deeds in our lives—perhaps not in the ways that we expect but, nevertheless, in ways we can trust.

Questions for Discussion or Reflection

1. What are some moments in your life when you have felt disappointed in the Lord for not meeting your expectations?

2. What are some moments of God's faithfulness in your life?

3. How can you be the evidence of God's faithfulness in someone else's life this season?

Gifts for the King

Share your stories of God's faithfulness with someone who does not know him.

Daily Blessing

Great is the LORD, and greatly to be praised; his greatness is unsearchable. On the glorious splendor of your majesty, and on your wondrous works, I will meditate.
—Psalm 145:3, 5, NRSV

You Who Are Poor

Monday, December 16, 2019

CHRISTINE

SCRIPTURES: Isaiah 55:1; Matthew 5:3; Luke 6:20

*Looking at his disciples, he said: "Blessed are you who are poor,
for yours is the kingdom of God."*
—Luke 6:20

Jesus loved the poor. There is no doubt about it. He called the poor blessed. He proclaimed good news to the poor. He commanded people to give to the poor and to invite them to their tables. There are dozens of verses in Scripture regarding the poor and how we are to treat them.

What is it about the poor that grabbed hold of the heart of Jesus? Why did he have such an affinity for them? And why would he call them blessed?

All are welcome at his table, but the Lord extends a special invitation to the poor. In Isaiah 55:1, he invites those who have no money to come and eat. It is the very picture of the gospel: the faces of the poor, gathered around his banqueting table, feasting in the kingdom of God. Imagine the Lord's generous spread of rich food. He holds nothing back from his impoverished guests. They have never experienced this kind of abundance.

We often read passages like this and are comforted by the words of invitation. We see ourselves sitting among these guests, enjoying the Lord's favor. Perhaps, however, the Lord would much prefer that we consider whom to take with us to the table instead of reserving a spot for ourselves. It is true that we are all invited to come and partake of the Lord. But let us not neglect the high call to care for those in need. Jesus urges us to give generously to the poor—not the figuratively poor but the materially poor; those who are economically underprivileged. How much are we willing to give from our own storehouses?

One of pastors on our district had her church pass out burritos to people experiencing homelessness in their community. By the time they got to a fellow we'll call Edwin, they had run out of food. The pastor gave him a post-card instead that gave information about their upcoming Christmas worship service. Edwin showed up at church. He missed out on the burrito, but that night he experienced a spirit-filled worship gathering and, afterward, a potluck feast fit for a king. Some church members invited him to their home, where he was given a place to wash up and sleep. He now attends church regularly and is on the way to finding a job and his own apartment.

What a foretaste of the kingdom of heaven when the people of God partner in the restoration of God's creation; when the poor and lowly are lifted up and honored; when the homeless find a home in the family of God!

Whether you find yourself in want or in plenty this Christmas season, may you find ways to be a blessing to others and also to be blessed by the kingdom of God that is being revealed in our midst.

Questions for Discussion or Reflection

1. In what way do the poor inherit the kingdom of God?

2. What does it mean to be invited to the banqueting table of the Lord?

3. Whom can you bless this Christmas season, especially among those who are less fortunate than you?

Gifts for the King

Find ways to demonstrate radical generosity this Christmas. Gather a group of people to extend support and hospitality to those who are facing financial difficulties this season.

Daily Blessing

Here I am! I stand at the door and knock. If anyone hears my voice and opens the door, I will come in and eat with that person, and they with me.
—Revelation 3:20

Praise the Lord

Tuesday, December 17, 2019
CHRISTINE

SCRIPTURE: Psalm 146

I will praise the LORD all my life; I will sing praise to my God as long as I live.
—Psalm 146:2

Psalm 146, the first of the five hallelujah psalms found at the end of the book of Psalms, has long evoked a spirit of praise and worship in those who meditate on its words. The hallelujah psalms were often sung out as hymns that exalted the God who is faithful even in the midst of turmoil.

"Praise the LORD" is the call to worship found in the first and last verses. Praise the Lord—even when facing circumstances where the odds are stacked against you. Praise the Lord—because, time and time again, God can be trusted to move radically in your life, when nothing else around you can be trusted.

God is working in the lives of his people, and in this passage, we see his active presence in this fallen world where he is creating, liberating, sustaining, restoring, and protecting. When we sing out these words of declaration, it is not just a hope but also a great expectation that the glory of the Lord will break through the darkest places of our lives.

Pause to imagine, for a moment, the diversity of voices that might have lifted up these very words throughout history:

- King David, who is thought to have penned this psalm, a shared heritage of covenant relationship with the Lord. Out of this rich tradition of storytelling, David proclaims the faithfulness of God to his people as evidenced during the direst times.

- An uprising of brave Christians sang this psalm when gathering in Nazi Germany to sign the Barmen Declaration, a document that essentially drew a line that distinguished them from a corrupted body of German Protestant churches. They confronted the spirit of darkness with these words of hope and promise.
- Imprisoned Korean Christians like Esther Ahn Kim memorized chapters of the Bible and meditated on these words for comfort and strength while being tortured for their faith during a period of persecution from the Japanese in the 1930s and 1940s.
- African American slaves sang words of praise and lament to the Lord as a form of nonviolent protest against slavery and bondage. Negro spirituals were filled with psalmist themes of liberation such as those found in Psalm 146, and it did much to fill their anguished hearts with hope, comfort, and dignity.

It is difficult to appreciate the power and passion behind these words from a privileged vantage point. The words of Psalm 146, read in a spirit of true worship, cannot help but incite a revolution of God's almighty love.

It may serve us well to read the psalmist's words afresh, through the eyes of the marginalized, the persecuted, the downtrodden, the person of color, the impoverished, the exploited, the stranger, the woman. Some of us may gain a much-needed, new perspective on the ways God is calling his people to partner in his restorative work and bring the hope of the gospel to the world.

Questions for Discussion or Reflection

1. How does reading Scripture from perspectives different than your own help you to see a fuller picture of the gospel?

2. How did the different perspectives represented in today's devotional deepen your appreciation of this passage? What did you learn about God?

Gifts for the King

Make a list of people you know who would broaden your understanding on how to interpret Scripture from different perspectives. Set aside some time to engage in meaningful conversations with them.

_____

_____

_____

_____

_____

_____

_____

_____

_____

_____

Daily Blessing

So do not fear, for I am with you; do not be dismayed, for I am your God. I will strengthen you and help you; I will uphold you with my righteous right hand.
—Isaiah 41:10

To Do Good Works

Wednesday, December 18, 2019

CHRISTINE

SCRIPTURES: Ephesians 2:8–10; James 2:14–19

For we are God's handiwork, created in Christ Jesus to do good works, which God prepared in advance for us to do.
—Ephesians 2:10

Decades before Albert and I started serving at our last church assignment, the church experienced an exodus of Baby Boomers that was caused by the legalism that characterized our denomination (as well as many others) at the time. Holiness was understood to be a (long) list of things believers weren't allowed to do: no dancing, no reading the newspaper on Sunday, no going to the movie theater, and so on. These were a few of the many regulations that frustrated those who left the church. Our understanding and practice of holiness has evolved over time, but for those who left, it was too little, too late. They had no desire to return.

The exodus also ended up wounding the congregants who stayed. They became sensitive toward anything that smelled like legalism. Some might have erred a little too far in the opposite direction, embracing the gospel of grace and feeling little urgency to act out their faith with deeds. We were saved by grace, a gift of God, were we not?

A study of the book of James reveals that yes, salvation is a gift from God that cannot be earned—but James declares that faith without deeds is dead. Our Wesleyan understanding of holiness naturally leads us to good works as a response to God's grace. God certainly gives us enough grace for our own benefit, but God also pours out his grace in such abundance that his love overflows in us, spilling over into the lives of others. God's grace changes us from the inside out, making us more like Jesus. Love begets love.

John Wesley's experience of God's love drove him to heartfelt works of hospitality toward God's people. For Wesley, to have faith meant to love as Jesus loved and to do what Jesus did. To be sanctified meant to be fully saturated in and motivated by God's unconditional love for us. Wesley practiced what he preached. His ministry to the poor and marginalized was marked with compassion and selflessness. Even in his old age, when most people settle comfortably into retirement, Wesley continued to serve the poor. His bones aching, he walked through the wintry streets to collect alms for the poor. He gave the clothing off his own back and denied himself any excess foods so that the hungry would benefit. For Wesley, as it should be for us, faith and deeds were inseparable.

Questions for Discussion or Reflection

1. In what ways have you been influenced by legalism in the church? In what ways have you displayed a legalistic attitude toward others?

2. Reread today's Scripture passages. There are some who claim that these two passages contradict each other. Explain how they might actually complement each other.

3. How will you express your worship and love for Jesus through acts of compassion toward others?

Gifts for the King

Spend some time with the Lord meditating on the love he has for you. Let that be the source that drives you to carry on the work of the Lord here on earth.

Daily Blessing

Teach me to do your will, for you are my God; may your good Spirit lead me on level ground.
—Psalm 143:10

The Least of These

Thursday, December 19, 2019
CHRISTINE

SCRIPTURES: Matthew 25:34–40; Luke 10:25–37

The King will reply, "Truly I tell you, whatever you did for one of the least of these brothers and sisters of mine, you did for me."
—Matthew 25:40

There is much scholarly discourse on the identity of the people described as "the least of these" in Matthew 25:40, and it's reasonable to assume this group includes the poor, the dispossessed, the marginalized, the sick. The mandate to care for those in need is repeated throughout Scripture. However, others claim that a more precise interpretation is that "the least of these" refers to Christian brothers and sisters who find themselves in vulnerable circumstances due to their obedience in spreading the gospel. Jesus knew the hardships his followers would face. He knew they would often depend on the mercy of others. Perhaps this is why Jesus said, "*I* was hungry," and "*I* was thirsty," and "*I* was a stranger"—because the least of these were fellow members of the body of Christ. When we read the parable through this interpretive lens, we hear a different invitation from Jesus: *be the least of these.*

When we vulnerably share our needs and invite others to come forward to meet those needs, we give them an opportunity to be blessed by the Father. There are some—especially those of us who are called to be shepherds and caregivers—for whom this is difficult to do. For some it is easier to be the giver, the provider, the visitor, than to be on the receiving end of another's generosity.

The parable of the Good Samaritan echoes these sentiments. It was the Jew—the insider—who was beaten and robbed, lying on the side of the road. And the Samaritan—the "other," the "hated one"—came to help, showing radical and unexpected generosity. There is no denying that Jesus told this parable to teach us to show radical hospitality, even toward those who hate us. But I wonder if another perspective could teach us something more. How many times have we read that story and identified with the Samaritan? We immediately place ourselves in the role of the charitable one, the humble humanitarian. But Jesus—a Jew—was speaking to other Jews. His listeners would be prompted to identify themselves as the victim on the side of the road—or, worse, the sidestepping priest or Levite.

What could we learn by taking on the identity of the injured Jew? Could we learn something by being the neighbor others can love? Being the stranger others can invite in? Being the wounded one others can heal? Perhaps there are circumstances when accepting the help of others leads to good things.

I have found that the potential of a relationship is limited if only one party is continually giving while the other is continually receiving. As a pastor, I was usually the one serving. But when I allowed others to serve me in my time of need, the relationship always seemed to rise to a new level. As a result, our friendship grew stronger, as did the body of Christ.

May the Lord grant you the humility and the courage to receive, as well as to give, this Advent season.

Questions for Discussion or Reflection

1. Do you find it difficult to receive love or assistance from others? Why is that?

2. When have you ever been "the least of these?" How did you feel when you allowed others to help you?

3. It is easy to see how showing hospitality and generosity to others is a form of Christian witness. But how is being the stranger or the neighbor in need also a form of witness?

Gifts for the King

Allow the King to love you through the hands and feet of someone else. Receive, and thank the Lord for his faithfulness.

Daily Blessing

You did not choose me, but I chose you and appointed you so that you might go and bear fruit—fruit that will last—and so that whatever you ask in my name the Father will give you. This is my command: Love each other.
—John 15:16-17

Offer Hospitality

Friday, December 20, 2019

ALBERT

SCRIPTURES: Luke 14:12-14; Hebrews 13:1-2; 1 Peter 4:7-11

Keep on loving one another as brothers and sisters. Do not forget to show hospitality to strangers, for by so doing some people have shown hospitality to angels without knowing it.
—Hebrews 13:1-2

The dinner table has long been a symbol of community. When we invite others into our homes and break bread together, we are saying, "You are welcome here. You are family." We cannot share our lives with each other without at some point sharing a meal.

For the believer, however, hospitality is more than inviting one's family and friends over for dinner. Jesus once said to his disciples, "If you greet only your own people, what are you doing more than others? Do not even pagans do that?" (Matthew 5:47). Rather, Christian hospitality is one of the ways we carry out the ministry of reconciliation. Inviting strangers and even our enemies to break bread with us is a subversive act of peace-making. As a friend once remarked to me, "We lay down our weapons in order to eat."

Hospitality is not so much about what we do as it is about whom we do it with. The early church stood out as a place where former rivals became family. Jews and gentiles worshiped together, ate together, prayed together, studied together, and served together. They sold property and possessions to give to anyone who had need. They met together daily in the temple courts and in each other's homes. People took notice, and God added to their number daily those who were being saved (see Acts 2:42-47).

God sanctifies his people as they practice hospitality. We learn to carry each other's burdens, to give and receive love, and to serve joyfully without expectation of reward. When we offer our homes and resources for God's use, we acknowledge that we are merely stewards, not owners, of God's property. In other words, practicing hospitality is one of the means by which we are formed into the likeness of Christ.

Over the years, Christine and I have invited hundreds of people into our home. The sounds of prayer and singing in different languages have often filled the house. People have been physically and emotionally healed in our living room. Marriages have been restored. The gospel has been shared at our dinner table. Our children have watched people take their first steps toward Jesus. Our home has often become a place of shelter and refuge. Once, we even provided temporary lodging for a young couple who had just returned from the hospital after the birth of their first child.

"Offer hospitality to one another without grumbling," the apostle Peter wrote. "Each of you should use whatever gift you have received to serve others, as faithful stewards of God's grace in its various forms" (1 Peter 4:9–10). Whom will you invite to your table this Advent season? How will you use your God-given gifts to serve others? How can you carry out the ministry of reconciliation in your own home?

Questions for Discussion or Reflection

1. How do people in your culture show hospitality? What have you observed about how hospitality is expressed differently in other cultures?

2. Who would be surprised by an invitation to dinner in your home? How can you extend hospitality as a means of healing a broken relationship? How is hospitality an expression of the ministry of reconciliation?

3. Each of us should use whatever gifts we have received to serve others, as faithful stewards of God's grace in its various forms (1 Peter 4:10). What gifts has God given you, and how can you use them to serve others during Advent?

Gifts for the King

Take some time to tidy up your home to make it a warm and inviting place for guests. As you do so, pray that God would make your home a place where the lonely are loved, the hurting are healed, and strangers becomes friends.

Daily Blessing

Whoever dwells in the shelter of the Most High will rest in the shadow of the Almighty. I will say of the LORD, "He is my refuge and my fortress, my God, in whom I trust."
—Psalm 91:1–2

Responding to the King

Saturday, December 21, 2019

Look over your notes and highlights from this week's devotionals. What do you sense God saying to you? How do you think God is asking you to respond? What evidence do you see of God's activity in your life this week? Take some time to write a letter of response and thanksgiving to the Lord as an act of worship and devotion.

Dear Heavenly Father,

Daily Blessing

May the God who gives endurance and encouragement give you the same attitude of mind toward each other that Christ Jesus had, so that with one mind and one voice you may glorify the God and Father of our Lord Jesus Christ.
—Romans 15:5-6

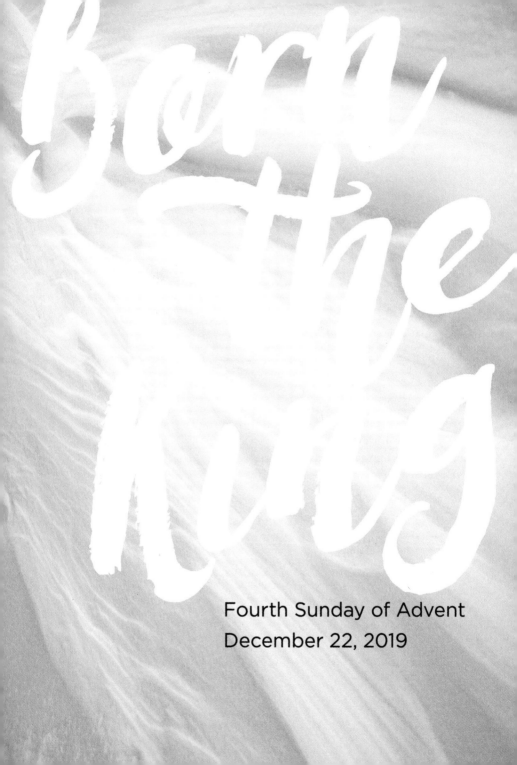

Fourth Sunday of Advent
December 22, 2019

Congregational Prayer

(Leader/**Everyone**)

O Lord, our God, O Christ, our brother,
We have gathered in your most holy name,
That we might drink together from the water of life.

We come to praise you, for you are Lord of all creation,
To enjoy you, for you are our heavenly Father,
To learn from you, for you are our wonderful Counselor,
And to serve you, for you are our almighty King.

Lord, we celebrate your coming,
In the flesh at Bethlehem,
In our hearts daily,
And in glory at the end of time.

Open up the floodgates of heaven, Lord;
Let streams of living water flow through our churches and our cities
As we seek to love our neighbors as you have loved us,
Showing ourselves to be your disciples.

Come, Lord Jesus.

Amen

This Is How

Sunday, December 22, 2019
ALBERT

SCRIPTURE: Matthew 1:18-25

This is how the birth of Jesus the Messiah came about: His mother Mary was pledged to be married to Joseph, but before they came together, she was found to be pregnant through the Holy Spirit.
—Matthew 1:18

The Bible is the story of God and God's people. It is not *a* book but a *library* of books, a collection of stories, songs, poems, historical records, letters, and prophecies written by dozens of authors over hundreds of years. All these writings have one thing in common: someone saw, heard, or experienced something that bore witness to the presence and power of God and decided it was a story worth repeating.

Each time we read Scripture, we should ask, "What is the story that is unfolding here, and why did these people think it ought to be told, retold, and ultimately written down?" A good follow-up question is, "How does my story fit into the larger story of God and humanity?"

The Gospel of Matthew begins with a story: "This is how the birth of Jesus the Messiah came about" (1:18). Mary is pledged to be married to Joseph, but before they come together, he learns that she is pregnant. Not wanting to expose her to public disgrace, he plans to divorce her quietly. But an angel of the Lord appears to Joseph in a dream, saying, "Joseph son of David, do not be afraid to take Mary home as your wife, because what is conceived in her is from the Holy Spirit. She will give birth to a son, and you are to give him the name Jesus, because he will save his people from their sins" (vv. 20–21).

It's not surprising that people thought the birth of the long-awaited Messiah was a story worth telling. What is striking, however, is the honesty and candor with which it is told. Mary is afraid. Joseph is embarrassed. Zechariah is skeptical. When God reveals that we are about to play a significant role in his story, we often react in similar ways. We are not certain if we are hearing the Lord correctly. We worry about what others might think. We feel that perhaps God might be better off choosing someone else to do the job. But God says, "Don't be afraid. What I am conceiving in your life is from the Holy Spirit. I am about to do something extraordinary through you. Will you trust me?"

Many religions have some kind of outward symbol to identify their followers. Hindus place markings on their foreheads (bindi). Jews wear skullcaps (yarmulke). Muslim women wear head coverings (hijab). Sikh men wear turbans. In fact, Christianity is the world's only major religion that does not suggest or require its members to wear any special marking or clothing. Instead, we identify ourselves as followers of Jesus by our stories—stories of reinvention, redemption, and renewal; stories about how the love of God has inspired and transformed us so that we love like God loves.

When it comes to writing your life story, who's holding the pen: you or God? What might happen if we surrender control of our lives to Jesus? What miracles might he choose to do through us? God wants your life to be a story worth repeating. Are you ready for the next chapter?

Questions for Discussion or Reflection

1. In your own words, what is the story of God?

2. Write down a timeline of the major turning points in your life story. At what points do you feel God may have been trying to get your attention and influence the direction of your life?

Gifts for the King

Choose one of the major turning points in your timeline that was especially transformative for you. What were the circumstances? How did you grow from the experience? Share the story with a friend or acquaintance today.

Daily Blessing

Don't you know that you yourselves are God's temple and that God's Spirit dwells in your midst?
—1 Corinthians 3:16

On His Shoulders

Monday, December 23, 2019

ALBERT

SCRIPTURE: Isaiah 9:2-7

For to us a child is born, to us a son is given, and the government will be on his shoulders. And he will be called Wonderful Counselor, Mighty God, Everlasting Father, Prince of Peace.
—Isaiah 9:6

What may sound like good news to one person can sometimes be bad news for another. Every time a country elects a new president, it seems like half the people cheer while the other half grumble. But when Christ was born, an angel of the Lord appeared to shepherds living out in the nearby fields and said, "Do not be afraid. I bring you good news that will cause great joy for *all* the people" (Luke 2:10, emphasis added).

The good news of the gospel is not only that Jesus is Savior but also that he is Lord. Christ is not only our brother; he is also our King. In a time when trust in our human leaders erodes further with each passing day, the news that the government ultimately rests upon the Messiah's shoulders should fill us with confidence and hope. The yoke of the oppressed will soon be shattered. Swords will be beaten into plowshares. The hungry shall be filled, and the meek shall inherit the earth. Christ "will reign on David's throne and over his kingdom, establishing and upholding it with justice and righteousness from that time on and forever" (Isaiah 9:7b).

God's plan is not to evacuate Christians one day while the rest of the world burns. God intends to restore all creation and live in it with us. This is truly good news for all people, everywhere.

Does the gospel we preach sound like good news to everyone—to the strong *and* the weak, the rich *and* the poor, the privileged *and* the disadvantaged alike? If not, then perhaps we do not fully understand the message and mission of Jesus. Whom do you know who needs to hear some good news for a change? How can you help them trust that God sees them in their distress and that help is on the way? Christ is seated at the right hand of the Father. He carries the world on his shoulders. Soon, our King will return, and "of the greatness of his government and peace there will be no end" (Isaiah 9:7a).

Questions for Discussion or Reflection

1. What is some of the best news you've ever received?

2. When did you first hear the gospel of Jesus Christ, and how was it explained to you? How has your understanding of the gospel changed or matured over time?

3. The prophet Isaiah wrote that the government would rest upon the Messiah's shoulders. What feelings or response does this promise stir in you?

Gifts for the King

Call, email, or text a friend for no other reason than to share some good news with them. Then ask your friend how you can be praying for them today.

Daily Blessing

The Son is the radiance of God's glory and the exact representation of his being, sustaining all things by his powerful word. After he had provided purification for sins, he sat down at the right hand of the Majesty in heaven.
—Hebrews 1:3

By His Son

Tuesday, December 24, 2019
ALBERT

SCRIPTURE: Hebrews 1:1–12

In the past God spoke to our ancestors through the prophets at many times and in various ways, but in these last days he has spoken to us by his Son, whom he appointed heir of all things, and through whom also he made the universe.
—Hebrews 1:1–2

Every day, in every corner of the world, human beings seek to communicate with the divine. Through prayer, ritual, supplication, and sacrifice, people seek help and guidance from a higher power. But all healthy relationships require mutual dialogue and shared life. When we speak to God, does God speak back? When we ask for help, does God respond? How do we know what God is thinking? How can we be sure God is listening?

The writer of Hebrews explains, "In the past God spoke to our ancestors through the prophets at many times and in various ways, but in these last days he has spoken to us by his Son, whom he appointed heir of all things, and through whom also he made the universe" (1:1–2). If we want to know what God is thinking, we can listen to the words of Jesus. If we want to know what God is like, we can look at the character of Jesus. If we want to know whether God responds to our cries for help, we can look at the actions of Jesus. "The Son is the radiance of God's glory and the exact representation of his being" (v. 3a). Jesus came into the world so that we might know God and share in the life of the Father, Son, and Holy Spirit.

One of the simplest definitions of a disciple of Jesus is someone who hears God's voice and does what God says. But God speaks more often in whispers than in shouts. To hear God's voice, we must draw away from the crowds, filter out the noise of the world, and learn to give God our undivided attention.

There is something about childbirth that invites us into this kind of sacred space. The minutes that followed the birth of each of our four children were holy moments. Time seemed to stand still as we held them in our arms. All our worries seemed a world away. We were fully immersed in the moment, wholly consumed with love. All was well with our souls.

Tonight, as evening falls, imagine what Mary must have been feeling on the night before Jesus's birth. Soon, she would be holding the Son of God in her arms. She would witness him draw his first breath; hear his first cry; nurse him at her breast for the first time; see his first smile; hear his first words; watch him take his first steps. One day, this child would grow up to be Mary's teacher, then her Savior, and finally her King. All her life, Mary would look upon the face of God and hear his voice.

How closely do you walk with Jesus? How well do you know him? Can you recognize his presence? Do you respond to his voice? Through Christ, we can have a direct, personal relationship with our Creator. God has given us his Son. This is what we celebrate on this holy night.

Questions for Discussion or Reflection

1. What are some ways you can develop your ability to hear from the Lord and be more spiritually discerning?

2. Have you ever felt as though God was clearly speaking to you? How did you recognize God's voice? What did God say, and how did you respond?

Gifts for the King

As evening falls, take a moment to listen to your favorite Christmas hymns. Pay close attention to the words of the songs and allow God to fill your heart with peace, hope, and joy. Offer a prayer of praise and thanksgiving to God. If you are spending Christmas Eve with family or friends, invite them to share this experience with you.

Daily Blessing

For there is one God and one mediator between God and mankind, the man Christ Jesus, who gave himself as a ransom for all people.
—1 Timothy 2:5-6a

Responding to the King

Wednesday, December 25, 2019

Look over your notes and highlights from this week's devotionals. What do you sense God saying to you? How do you think God is asking you to respond? What evidence do you see of God's activity in your life this week? Take some time to write a letter of response and thanksgiving to the Lord as an act of worship and devotion.

Dear Heavenly Father,

Daily Blessing

May the grace of the Lord Jesus Christ, and the love of God, and the fellowship of the Holy Spirit be with you all.
—2 Corinthians 13:14